He Gave Thanks:
An Introduction to
The Eucharistic Prayer

J.M.Smith
1994.

by

Geoffrey Cuming

Tutor of Ripon College, Cuddesdon, Oxford
Consultant Member of the Church of England Liturgical Commission

GROVE BOOKS

BRAMCOTE   NOTTS.

CONTENTS

ACKNOWLEDGMENTS

The quotations from the Psalter are taken from *The Psalms: A New Translation for Worship,* which is bound in with the ASB and entitled 'the Liturgical Psalter'. They are reprinted here by kind permission of Collins Liturgical Publications. The quotations from the Gloria in Excelsis and the Te Deum are from the 1974 ICET versions of these canticles.

THE COVER PICTURE

is by Peter Ashton

First Impression December 1981

ISSN 0306 0608

ISBN 0 907536 13 1

1. INTRODUCTION

'We follow his example and obey his command.' From the earliest times the Christian Church has obeyed Jesus' command by following his example at the Last Supper, and has continued to 'do this in remembrance' of him. There has been much scholarly argument about what Jesus meant, and even whether he actually said those words (since Mark does not mention them). But the earliest forms of service that have come down to us already quote the gospel accounts of the Last Supper or allude to a 'pattern which is from' him; and, ever since, makers of liturgy have assumed that the gospel narratives must form the starting-point of any communion service.

As Dom Gregory Dix pointed out in his influential book *The Shape of the Liturgy* (1945), in all four accounts of the Last Supper Jesus is represented as performing four actions with e bread: taking, giving thanks, breaking, and giving to the disciples; and similarly with the cup, though there is no action corresponding to breaking the bread. There were thus seven actions at the Last Supper; but all early liturgies telescope them into four, taking and giving thanks over the bread and the cup simultaneously, and delaying the breaking and distribution of the bread until the wine also has been consecrated. Only in recent times have any liturgies directed the distribution of the bread before the words over the cup have been said, which a literal following of the gospel accounts would require.

Not all four actions are of equal importance. 'Taking' is simply a preliminary to 'giving thanks', and is probably only mentioned to focus attention on thanksgiving: to say 'he took bread and gave thanks' is more vivid than 'he gave thanks over some bread'.[1] 'The breaking of the bread' is alluded to several times in Acts, though it is not certain whether this means an ordinary meal or the eucharist. Again, 'breaking', like 'taking', is a preparatory action, to make possible the distribution of the bread. Thus the two important actions are giving thanks and distributing, to which the others are subordinate. In this essay we shall concentrate on these two, tracing their development from the New Testament to the Alternative Service Book.

Many modern revisions have based their work on this New Testament foundation; almost all have taken the earliest liturgies as their models. This is particularly true of the Roman Catholic Church, the Church of England, and the Episcopal Church in America. So another purpose of this essay is to explain the relevance of the oldest liturgies to the newest, while taking a look in passing at the distortions of the Middle Ages and the reactions of the Reformers, with special reference to the Book of Common Prayer.

Before we go any further, those who are new to the subject must be introduced to some technical terms and to the liturgies mentioned in the essay; those who are familiar with these already should turn to page 5.

---

[1] J. Jeremias *The Eucharistic Words of Jesus* ([2]ET, 1966) pp.174-5.

The communion service is also known as 'the Eucharist' (which means 'thanksgiving'), and its central prayer as 'the eucharistic prayer'. These names are used in the new Roman and Anglican services. In the East the service is called 'the liturgy' and the prayer 'the anaphora' [offering]; in the West the corresponding terms were 'the Mass' and 'the Canon'; in the Book of Common Prayer, 'Holy Communion' and 'the Prayer of Consecration'. The liturgical account of the Last Supper is called 'the Institution Narrative', and is followed in most liturgies by 'the anamnesis' ['remembrance'], a section in which Christ's death and resurrection are 'remembered'. Invocation of the Holy Spirit on the elements or on the worshippers is called 'the epiclesis'. The first section of the prayer is called 'the Preface', which here means 'proclamation', not 'introduction'; and the prayer ends with 'the doxology', giving glory to God.

A very large number of eucharistic prayers of all ages have come down to us. Apart from two or three very early texts, most of the great liturgies took shape during the fourth century, but the earliest manuscripts date from 800 A.D. or later, by which time the texts have undergone a good deal of alteration. The early liturgies are each associated with one of the leading centres of Christianity; when they bear the name of a saint, it must not be assumed that he is the author, particularly in the case of one or all of the apostles.

EARLY LITURGIES

Addai and Mari	In parts, very early	East Syria
Apostolic Constitutions	Earliest complete service	West Syria
Cyril	350-386	Jerusalem
Didache	? 1st century	? Syria
Hippolytus	Earliest eucharistic prayer, c. 215	Rome
Justin Martyr	Earliest description of euchar-ist, c. 150	Rome
St. Basil	Earliest version, ? 300	Egypt (from Cappadocia?)
	Later version, c. 370	Constantinople
St. James	400+	Jerusalem
St. John Chrysostom	380+	Constantinople
St. Mark	Papyrus fragments, ? 2nd century	Alexandria
	Complete liturgy, ? 500	

CHURCH OF ENGLAND

Book of Common Prayer	1st edition, 1549
	2nd edition, much altered, 1552
	Final revision, 1662
Series 2	1967
Series 3	1973
Alternative Service Book, Rite A	1980

EPISCOPAL CHURCH OF THE USA

Book of Common Prayer	1979

ROMAN CATHOLIC CHURCH

Ordo Missae	1969

Having introduced the cast, we can now proceed to unfold the story.

2. BERAKAH

When Jesus gave thanks over the bread and the cup at the Last Supper, what did he say? This is one of the gaps in the gospel narratives which we should most like to see filled. But nobody has ever claimed to reproduce the exact words of Jesus on this occasion, either in a liturgy or in any other form of writing. One inference which has been drawn from this lacuna is that he simply used the appropriate current Jewish form, which was so familiar to all Jews that there was no need to quote the actual text.

For at least three centuries liturgical scholars carried on a search for a hypothetical single eucharistic prayer representing what Jesus said at the Last Supper, or at any rate, what he was believed to have said. From this all later eucharistic prayers would have been derived. Dom Gregory Dix, having suggested with considerable foe that the whole search had been a wild-goose-chase, nevertheless quotes a Jewish thanksgiving, with the comment:

'The traditional school have tended for some reason to ignore this series of "thanksgivings". But I will venture to prophesy that this will eventually prove to be their fortress, which the critics will be unable to capture.'[1]

Dix himself did not pursue this line of inquiry to any depth, being more concerned with establishing the primacy of the 'four actions', but his prophecy set other scholars to work. Two French liturgists, Louis Bouyer[2] and Louis Ligier[3], followed up Dix's hint, and, though working quite independently of each other, came to much the same conclusion. For both, the origin of the eucharistic prayer is to be found in the *Birkath ha-mazon,* or Blessing for Food, one of the Jewish table-prayers which Jesus may very well have used. It is in three sections:

1. Blessing of him who nourishes
Blessed are you, Lord our God, King of the universe, for you nourish us and the whole world with goodness, grace, kindness, and mercy.

Blessed are you, Lord, for you nourish the universe.

2. Blessing for the earth
We will give thanks to you, Lord our God, because you have given us for our inheritance a desirable land, good and wide, the covenant and the Law, life and food. And for all these things we give you thanks and bless your name for ever and beyond.

Blessed are you, Lord our God, for the earth and for food.

3. Blessing for Jerusalem
Have mercy, Lord our God, on us your people Israel, and your city Jerusalem, on your sanctuary and your dwellingplace, on Zion the habitation of your glory, and the great and holy house over which

[1] G. Dix *The Shape of the Liturgy* (1945) p.217.
[2] L. Bouyer *Eucharist* (ET, 1968) pp.50-135.
[3] L. Ligier, e.g. 'The Origins of the Eucharistic Prayer' in *Studia Liturgica* 9 (1963) pp.161-185.

your name is invoked. Restore the kingdom of the house of David to its place in our days, and speedily build Jerusalem. Blessed are you, Lord, for you build Jerusalem. Amen.

There is nowadays a fourth paragraph, Blessing of the Good and Beneficent, which need not be quoted, since there is general agreement that it is later than the first century A.D., and therefore does not come into the argument.

At first sight, this *Berakah* seems to have little in common with any Christian prayer. As far as purely verbal resemblance goes, this impression is correct. Despite the presence of one or two 'pre-echoes', the language does not immediately suggest a relationship. But if the structure, that is, the order of themes, is made the basis of comparison, a certain similarity becomes apparent. In the first paragraph of the *Birkath* God is blessed for creating and sustaining the world, and in the second, for giving his people food; and in the third, prayer is made for the restoration of Jerusalem. *Mutatis mutandis,* this could serve equally well as a précis of some of the earliest anaphoras, particularly those of SS. *Addai and Mari* and the Egyptian St. *Basil,* all of which go back to very early dates. In them, of course, the food has become the spiritual food of the eucharist, and Jerusalem has become the Christian Church.

If there is a genuine parentage here, and if Jesus's thanksgiving at the Last Supper was indeed based on this particular thanksgiving, or even merely followed the ordinary rules for the composition of *berakoth,* it will be well worth while to look at this characteristically Jewish prayer-form. An authoritative description is given by the Judaic scholar Ismar Elbogen:

'*Berakah* comes from *berakh,* which means originally "to fall on one's knees", then takes on the meaning "to intercede", "to bless", and finally "to praise or glorify God". So *berakah* means at once the prayer of praise and the giving of thanks; it has always the character of a hymn . . . Its prototype is the numerous prayers of praise in the Psalms, particularly the doxologies at the end of the different books of the Psalter.'[1]

The dividing line between *berakah* and *todah,* blessing and thanksgiving, is not easy to draw, and scholars are divided as to the extent to which it is possible to distinguish between them. Some indeed hold that they are indistinguishable; and this division of opinion is also found in relation to the New Testament equivalents *eulogein* and *eucharistein.* The same is true of such verbs as 'praise' and 'confess'.

The character of the *berakah* will be more clearly seen by taking Elbogen's hint and looking at some examples from familiar psalms, rather than from unfamiliar Jewish prayers. This opening is typical:

'O praise the Lord.
For it is good to sing praises to our God:
and to praise him is joyful and right.' (Psalm 147.1).

[1] *Der jüdische Gottesdienst in seiner geschichtlichen Entwicklung* ([3]1931) p.4 (my translation).

By the third century A.D., fixed rules had been laid down: it was obligatory to mention the name of God and his Kingdom. But this practice was obviously much older, as this example shows:
'I will exalt you, O God my king:
    I will bless your name for ever and ever.
Every day will I bless you:
    and praise your name for ever and over' (Psalm 145.1-2).

Every *berakah* had to end with a formula of blessing, and this rule applied even to those *berakoth* which included petitionary prayer, such as the *Eighteen Benedictions* of the daily synagogue prayers.

Thus the fundamental purpose of the *berekah* was to bless, praise, glorify, or give thanks to God, his kingdom, and his name. What then is the content of the blessing? For what is God blessed? One favourite theme is creation:
'Bless the Lord, O my soul:
    O Lord my God how great you are!
Clothed with majesty and honour:
    wrapped in light as a garment.
You have stretched out the heavens
like a tent-cloth . . .
you have set the earth on its foundations:
    so that it shall never be moved.
The deep covered it as with a mantle . . .' (Psalm 104.1-3, 6-7).
And so the psalmist goes on through the wonders of creation, the wild asses, the stork, the conies, Leviathan, and all the rest of them.

But this is only a beginning: God is a God who acts in the affairs of men. That is the implication of praising his name, which is done by commemorating his works:
'O give thanks to the Lord and call upon his name:
    tell among the peoples what things he has done.
Sing to him, O sing praises:
    and be telling of all his marvellous works . . .
Call to mind what wonders he has done:
    his marvellous acts and the judgments of his mouth.' (Psalm 105.1, 2, 5)

This time the psalmist goes on to recall the whole history of Israel, through Abraham, Isaac, and Jacob, Joseph and Moses, culminating in the rescue of God's people from slavery; and so redemption is often singled out as the greatest of God's works:
'O give thanks to the Lord, for he is good . . .
Let the Lord's redeemed say so:
    whom he has redeemed from the hand of the enemy.' (Psalm 107.1-2)

Or the *berakah* may take the form of a plea for rescue:
'Save us, O Lord our God and gather us from among the nations:
    that we may give thanks to your holy name
    and make our boast in your praises.' (Psalm 106.49).

Or the idea of redemption may be individualized:
'Praise the Lord, O my soul:
    and forget not all his benefits,
who forgives all your sin:
    and heals all your infirmities,
who redeems your life from the Pit (Psalm 103.2-4).

But always the remembrance is an active process, a proclamation rather than a mere recollection:
'Their lips shall flow
with the remembrance of your abundant goodness . . .
They speak of the glory of your kingdom:
and tell of your great might.' (Psalm 145.7, 11)

The themes of creation and redemption will later form the foundation of the great Christian anaphoras; but they already provide the chief subjects of thanksgiving in the Psalter.

The Christian Church was not slow to take over the Jewish themes. Christian *berakoth* are found in Revelation:
'You are worthy, O Lord our God, to receive glory and honour and power, because you created all things; by your will they were created and have their being. (Rev. 4.11).

The theme of creation is followed in the next chapter by that of redemption:
'You are worthy to take the scroll and to break its seals, for you were slain and by your blood did purchase for God men of every tribe and language, people and nation . . .'
'Worthy is the Lamb, the Lamb that was slain to receive all power and wealth, wisdom and might, honour and glory and praise!' (Rev. 5.9, 12).

Every created thing then joins in a doxology:
'Praise and honour, glory and might, to him who sits on the throne and to the Lamb for ever and ever!' (Rev. 5.13).

And the four living creatures answer, 'Amen'. It is a commonplace that these chapters present an idealized picture of the Sunday worship of the early Church.

Three hundred years later, the hymnody of the Church still took the same form and the same themes:
'You are God and we praise you:
you are the Lord and we acclaim you;
You are the eternal Father:
all creation worships you . . .
You, Christ, are the King of Glory:
the eternal Son of the Father.
When you became man to set us free:
you did not abhor the Virgin's womb . . .
Come then Lord and help your people:
bought with the price of your own blood . . .
Day by day we bless you:
and we praise your name . . .'

Or again:
'Glory to God in the highest . . .
we worship you we give you thanks:
we praise you for your glory . . .
you take away the sin of the world:
have mercy on us.'

After which, the canticle ends with a doxology.

3. EUCHARISTIA

In the psalms the two themes of creation and redemption appear separately; creation in Psalm 104, redemption in Psalm 103, and so on. This is still the case in the *Didache,* a very early document of markedly Jewish character:

'We give you thanks, holy Father, for your holy name . . . You, Lord almighty, created all things for the sake of your name, and gave food and drink to men for their enjoyment, that they might give you thanks.'[1]

But there is nothing about redemption. So too the earliest manuscript of the anaphora of *St. Mark* (the liturgy of Alexandria), which praises God

'who made heaven and all that is in it, the earth and what is on earth, seas, rivers, and all that is in them . . .
Your name is great among all nations.'[2]

But again there is no reference to redemption, and this rains a peculiarity of the fully developed anaphora of *St. Mark.* The anaphora used at Jerusalem in the time of St. Cyril is on similar lines, and adds sun, moon, and stars to the list of created things.

The combination of the two themes in one prayer is a Christian innovation. Around 135 A.D. Justin Martyr describes the president of the brethren sending up praise and glory to God

'both for creating the world with all things that are in it, and for freeing us from the evil in which we were born.'[3]

This outline is filled in by the anaphora of *SS Addai and Mari:*

'Worthy of glory from every mouth and thanksgiving from every tongue is the adorable and glorious name of the Father . . He created the world through his grace, and its inhabitants through his kindness; he saved men through his mercy, and gave great grace to mortals.'[4]

Almost the only other anaphora to give equal importance to both themes is that of the *Apostolic Constitutions* (?360-380 A.D.), which spends a whole page on giving thanks, among other things, for the heavens, the sun, moon and stars, for water, fire, the ocean, the dry land, the deeps and the heights, sweet-smelling herbs, the hissing of reptiles, the cries of variegated birds, and, finally, man. All this is the work of God the Father, who 'brought all things out of non-existence to existence' through the Son. The anaphora continues with a précis of the Old Testament from the Fall down to the capture of Jericho, followed by a brief account of the ministry of Jesus.[5] Nowhere else can one find so panoramic a thanksgiving.

---

[1] R. C. D. Jasper and G. J. Cuming (ed.) *Prayers of the Eucharist* ([2]1980) p.15; hereafter abbreviated as *PEER.* References are given to both the first (1975) and second editions, except where the pagination is the same (pp.1-28).
[2] *PEER* [1]p.38, [2]p.43.
[3] *PEER* p.17.
[4] *PEER* p.27.
[5] *PEER* [1]p.67, [2]p.72.

The thanksgiving for creation developed in two ways, each of which tended to alter its character. One way is found in the later Jerusalem liturgy of *St. James,* which begins the anaphora:
> 'It is truly fitting and right . . . to bless you, to worship you, to glorify you, to give thanks to you, the creator of all creation;'

and then goes on:
> 'The heavens hymn you . . . the sun and the moon and all the choirs of the stars, earth and sea, and all that is in them; the heavenly Jerusalem . . .'[1]

Here it is not the Church giving thanks to God for having created the world, but the whole of creation itself that praises God for having created it. This approach also has its roots in the Psalter:
> 'Praise him, sun and moon:
> > praise him, all you stars of light.
>
> Praise him you highest heaven:
> > and you waters that are above the heavens.
>
> Let them praise the name of the Lord:
> > for he commanded and they were made.' (Psalm 148.3-5).

The canticle *Benedicite* from the Septuagint works out this idea at even greater length. In Revelation all creation joins in with the heavenly host, but without any detail about its component parts. Similarly, the Byzantine version of *St. Basil* says only:
> 'The whole reasonable and intelligent creation does you service and renders you unending praise and glory.'[2]

St. John Chrysostom is even more reticent, contenting itself with merely quoting the Syrian phrase mentioned above, 'You brought us out of non-existence'.[3] In these liturgies the emphasis is moving from what God *does* to what he *is.*

The second development took place under the influence of such passages as John 1.2-3 and Colossians 1.16, which attribute the work of creation to the Son as well as the Father. This appears at a very early date; already in the *Apostolic Tradition* of Hippolytus (*c.* 215):
> 'We render thanks to you, O God, through your beloved child Jesus Christ . . . through whom you made all things.'[4]

That is all that Hippolytus has to say about creation, whereas he spreads himself on the incarnation and the atonement. Similarly the Egyptian version of *St. Basil* runs:
> 'you made heaven and earth and the sea and all that is in them. Father of our Lord . . . Jesus Christ, through whom you made all things visible and invisible.'[5]

The first sentence is probably due to Egyptian influence (see *St. Mark,* above): the second may well be due to St. Basil himself, who several

---

[1] *PEER* [1]p.56, [2]p.61.
[2] *PEER* [1]p.84, [2]p.98.
[3] *PEER* [1]p.79, [2]p.89.
[4] *PEER* p.22.
[5] *PEER* [1]p.30, [2]p.35.

times criticizes the tendency of the liturgy to dwell on created things and recommends concentrating instead on the history of our salvation.[1] In any case, once the theme of creation was associated with the Son, it was bound to be subordinated to that of redemption, and deprived of its rich content.

From this development it is only a short step to discarding any mention of creation at all, and this step was in fact taken in the West. The Roman Canon specifies no reasons for thanksgiving in the *invariable* part of the Preface, but confines the utterance of praise to the events of our redemption, set out in instalments following the course of the liturgical year. The worshippers pray for their voices to be admitted, but creation appears neither as the subject nor the agent of praise. Even in the East, where *some* reference to creation, however minimal, was still *de rigueur,* the tendency was to place the main emphasis on the history of redemption. In *St. John Chrysostom,* however, the standard 'Orthodox Liturgy', the theme of redemption is confined to the quotation of the single verse John 3.16. Thus in the two great liturgies of East and West, which held undisputed primacy for over a thousand years in their respective churches, thanksgiving both for creation and for redemption was sadly whittled away compared with the full treatment which both themes had received in the early centuries.

---

[1] J. P. Migne *Patrologia Graeca* 31, pp.253C, 913A, 1329A.

11

4. LATER DEVELOPMENTS

In parallel with the downgrading of thanksgiving, and no doubt interacting with it, was a tendency to transfer the venue of thanksgiving from earth to heaven. This was achieved by the introduction of the Sanctus. Originating in the East, it seems not to have reached Rome, always intensely conservative in liturgical matters, until about the year 450. Dix rightly describes it as 'a sort of liturgical cuckoo, which ends by taking the place of the "thanksgivings" whenever it is admitted into the prayer'.[1] At Rome it led to the total severance of the Preface from the rest of the Canon, which thereafter lacked any element of thanksgiving at all. In medieval thought the Preface and Sanctus together have become a single independent unit and the eucharistic prayer begins, following them, at *Te igitur.* In the East, however, this complete separation of the thanksgiving section has never taken place. There are other consequences of the introduction of the Sanctus: once the earthly offering of thanks has been linked in this way with the worship of the heavenly host, it is only a short step to the concept of the heavenly altar, and the descent of the Holy Spirit upon the earthly worshippers and their offering, as found in the great medieval liturgies.

Cranmer inherited this situation of the separation of the Sanctus from the Canon, and proceeded to make it worse by reducing the number of proper prefaces and of the days on which each was said. He did, at least temporarily, provide thanksgiving for the lives of the saints in the 1549 Canon, but even this disappeared in 1552, and the only invariable element of thanksgiving in the latter service is the post-communion collect. The Preface to the Sanctus continues to remind us that 'it is very meet, right, and our bounden duty' to give thanks to God, but on only thirty-two days in the year does it specify what we are to give God thanks for. This seems to have been quite deliberate on Cranmer's part. As is well known, he used a lot of material from the Church Order for Cologne (known in England as 'Hermann's *Consultation*'). This contains a Preface of decidedly Eastern character, beginning with a brief thanksgiving for creation, and proceeding through the fall, the incarnation, and the atonement before leading into the Sanctus.[2] Cranmer completely ignored this Preface, and instead abbreviated the Roman Preface. In 1552 he detached the Sanctus even further from the rest of the eucharistic prayer by inserting the Prayer of Humble Access between them. Thanksgiving seems to have been his blind spot: there is none in Morning or Evening Prayer either, despite the statement in the opening exhortation that we have met together 'to render thanks for the great benefits that we have received at his hands'. A similar lacuna follows the quotation from 1 Timothy about giving thanks for all men at the beginning of the Prayer for the Church Militant, though this was remedied in 1662. Even in the post-communion collect thanksgiving is not for creation and redemption, but for the benefits of communion.

[1] *The Shape of the Liturgy* p.219.
[2] *PEER* [1]p.145, [2]p.159.

The revision of 1662 only widened the gap after the Sanctus by introducing the title 'The Prayer of Consecration', as though the thanksgiving of the Preface and the Sanctus had nothing to do with consecration. Despite their respect for the ancient liturgies, the Caroline divines had little real understanding of them, though in the General Thanksgiving written by Bishop Reynolds in 1661, which there is some reason to believe was originally a eucharistic prayer, we bless God 'for our creation, preservation, and all the blessings of this life, but above all, for the redemption of the world by our Lord Jesus Christ'. This exactly reflects the subject matter and the priorities of the oldest liturgies. The amateur liturgists of the seventeenth and early eighteenth centuries had a deeper insight into the theology of the Eastern liturgies, and accordingly included some degree of thanksgiving in their unofficial productions, such as the liturgies of the eighteenth century Nonjurors. Strangely enough, their lead was not followed in this matter by the Scottish Episcopalians, who took them as their model at so many other points, and who possessed in Thomas Rattray one of the foremost liturgical scholars of the century, editor of a critical edition of *St. James.*

Neither the Church of England nor the Roman Catholic Church made any changes at all in their liturgies during the nineteenth century. In 1927-28 the Church of England made some attempt to remedy this particular deficiency of the Prayer Book service. Under the influence of W. H. Frere, the Prayer of Humble Access was moved elsewhere, and the Prayer of Consecration was linked to the Sanctus by the addition of the words 'All glory be to thee' at the beginning; this also had the effect of restoring a thanksgiving for redemption. But the prayer never came into any general use.

Thirty years later, when the Church of England Liturgical Commission began to revise the communion service, the dominant influence on liturgists of all countries was that of Hippolytus. Dix's edition of the *Apostolic Tradition,* which appeared in 1937, was accepted as having established a trustworthy text of the earliest anaphora known to us, and the two later editions by Dom Bernard Botte had placed the anaphora on an even securer footing. Accordingly, the Series 2 communion service has a substantial 'Thanksgiving' (so entitled), which like that of Hippolytus, is almost entirely Christocentric:

'Because through him thou hast created all things from the beginning, and fashioned us men in thine own image;

through him thou didst redeem us from the slavery of sin, giving him to be born as man, to die upon the cross, and to rise again for us.'

The inclusion of creation among the works of Christ has been criticized by J. L. Houlden, who writes:

'We appeal thereby to a biblical and patristic concept, that of Christ as the pre-existent Logos, which is more remote from

13

present-day thought than almost any other, and which is so far removed from readily accessible imagery that its evocative power is minimal, except for the initiated. Hardly one worshipper in thousands can be expected to find in it an appropriate expression of his faith.'[1]

If the revisers had gone back *behind* Hippolytus to Jewish tradition, they would have gone far to forestall this particular criticism. Few modern liturgies display the Jewish delight in the variety of creation, a genuinely biblical insight which would balance our present preoccupation with man and with Christology.

The Series 2 Thanksgiving also ran into difficulty by including the whole of salvation history *before* the Sanctus, a mistake avoided by all the Eastern liturgies. This produces exactly the same effect as that from which the historic Roman Canon and the Prayer Book suffer, of breaking off the first section of the eucharistic prayer from the remainder, thus giving the impression of a thanksgiving and a prayer independent of each other (this though typographically it looks like one prayer). Where the ancient liturgies simply continue after the Sanctus with the mighty works of Christ, Series 2 has to make a fresh start with an abrupt change of subject-matter:

'. . . **Glory be to thee, O Lord most high.**
Hear us, O Father, though Christ thy Son our Lord . . .'

Series 3 did little to improve matters, though it did try to forge some sort of link with the words 'Accept our praises'. This, however, is still petition, not thanksgiving. Admittedly salvation history is not neglected elsewhere in Series 2 and 3. By the inclusion of the passion, resurrection, and ascension, before the Sanctus, a feeling of repetition is inevitably created after the Institution Narrative, where these events are traditionally enumerated (twice in Series 3, with the acclamation 'Christ has died . . .'!). Finally, the Preface of these services duplicates the Creed, though this problem is best solved by omitting the Creed as a comparatively late arrival in the eucharist and now superfluous.

Modern liturgies vary in their handling of the Sanctus: the American Prayer C gets as far as the incarnation before the Sanctus, while Prayer B only starts its invariable thanksgiving with creation after the Sanctus. The latter procedure, which is also adopted by Canada, Ireland, and Wales, perpetuates the separation of the Sanctus from the Thanksgiving, but much less drastically than 1662. The Roman Prayer III also follows this pattern (Prayers I and II, which are simply adaptations of the medieval Canon and of Hippolytus respectively, share the characteristics of their models). But Prayer IV, which is based on Eastern and Gallican models (and is paraphrased in the American Prayer D) at last gives us a satisfactorily constructed modern Thanksgiving in the form of the great ancient liturgies. Here is the opening section:

'Father in heaven, it is right that we should give you thanks and glory: you alone are God, living and true. Through all eternity you

---

[1] 'Liturgy and her Companions' in R. C. D. Jasper (ed.) *The Eucharist Today* (1974) p.173.

live in unapproachable light. Source of life and goodness, you have created all things, to fill your creatures with every blessing and lead all men to the joyful vision of your light. In the name of every creature under heaven, we too praise your glory.'

Then comes the Sanctus, after which the prayer proceeds:

'Further, we acknowledge your greatness: all your actions show your wisdom and love. You formed man in your own likeness . . . Even when he disobeyed you . . . you did not abandon him to the power of death . . . Again and again you offered a covenant to man, and through the prophets taught him to hope for salvation.

Father, you so loved the world that in the fullness of time you sent your only Son to be our Saviour . . . To the poor he proclaimed the good news of salvation, to prisoners freedom, and to those in sorrow joy. In fulfilment of your will he gave himself up to death; but by rising from the dead, he destroyed death and restored life.'

(A few phrases have been left out, to make the main themes stand out more clearly.) In this eloquent prayer creation and redemption are presented in two stages, divided by the Sanctus, in one all-embracing purpose, and the whole forms the subject of the Church's thanksgiving. It is perhaps the only recent prayer to recapture the grandeur and sweep, combined with clear structure, of *St. Basil* or *St. James,* and thus to introduce to the Western Church a new dimension for its eucharistic prayers.

This return to the earliest discoverable procedures is no mere archaeological investigation. If that were all, the laborious and time-consuming process of revision would not have been justified by the results. As it is, the West has recovered a deep insight into the essentials of worship which the East has never lost.

5. CONSECRATION

So far we have been considering the background and content of the thanksgiving: the next question is, what was thought to be its effect? Origen (c. 250) says:
'We give thanks to the Creator of the universe and eat the loaves that are presented with thanksgiving and prayer over the gifts so that by the prayer they become a certain holy body.'[1]

This is in line with Justin's account quoted above, but Justin himself suggests that the thanksgiving should include a 'word' of Jesus:
'We have been taught that the food over which thanks have been given by a word of prayer that is from him . . . is both the flesh and the blood of (the) incarnate Jesus.'[2]

(The Greek for 'a word of prayer' is ambiguous, but I am convinced that this is the correct translation; similarly, 'from him' could refer to God the Father or to Jesus, both of whom have been referred to earlier in the sentence, but 'Jesus' seems more probable.) Justin was writing c. 150, but the words 'we have been taught' show that this belief was already held a generation earlier. A little later than Justin, Irenaeus writes:
'When the mixed cup and the created bread receive the word of God, they become *eucharistia,* the body and blood of Christ.'[3]

All these writers believe that the bread and wine become the body and blood of Christ as a result of thanksgiving; but what is the word of Jesus or of God which has this effect? Almost certainly, the words of Jesus at the Last Supper, which appear in all liturgies from at least the year 400. At first sight the Institution Narrative seems to have been added simply to certify that all was being done as the Lord had commanded. Cyprian (c. 250) lays down the principle that we should do in the eucharist 'what the Lord did'. This presumably includes saying what he said. Thus the presence of the Institution Narrative in the service, and even in the Thanksgiving, was perfectly natural, and need not have carried any further *doctrinal* implications. Perhaps the Liturgy of *St. Mark* brings this out most clearly:
'With all that hallow you, receive also . . . our hallowing . . . Fill, O God, this sacrifice also with a blessing from you . . . Because our Lord . . . Jesus the Christ, in the night when he handed himself over, took bread . . .'[4]

The word 'Because' carries much theological weight. It means that the narrative which follows provides the authority and historical warrant for our offering of thanks and our expectation of God's response in transforming the bread and wine; the Narrative is not yet seen as having the power of transformation in itself.

[1] *Contra Celsum* 8.33 (ET, H. Chadwick, p.476).
[2] *PEER* p.19; cf. G. J. Cuming 'Di'euches logou' in *Journal of Theological Studies* n.s. 31(1980) pp.80-2.
[3] *Adversus Haereses* 5.2.2.
[4] *PEER* [1]pp.47-8, [2]pp.52-3.

16

This is already hinted at in the quotations from Justin and Irenaeus above, but, striking as they are, it would be wrong to read into them the full medieval doctrine of transubstantiation. When Hippolytus, a generation later than Irenaeus, wants to describe the elements, he uses words like 'antitype' and 'likeness'; and these words still appear in the liturgies of *St. Basil* and Sarapion respectively, two hundred years after Justin. So too, Tertullian's word *'figura'* is still present in the liturgy of Milan at the end of the fourth century. Meanwhile, the thanksgiving which consecrates has been given a new meaning, already adumbrated in Justin, but now fully worked out.

When Ambrose, bishop of Milan from 374 to 397, comes to explain to his baptismal candidates what is meant by consecration, he uses realist language:
> 'Before it is consecrated, it is bread: but when the words of Christ are added, it is the body of Christ.'

Not, be it noted, 'the figure of the body', as his liturgy has it, but the body itself. He then says quite categorically,
> 'The word of Christ completes the sacrament.'[1]

By that time there was nothing unusual about this kind of language, particularly in the West. Ambrose's words just quoted recall his disciple Augustine's famous dictum,
> *'Accedit verbum ad elementum et fit sacramentum.'* ('The word is added to the element, and the result is the sacrament.')[2]

Here is the beginning of the medieval doctrine that consecration is effected, not by thanksgiving, but by the recitation of the word of Christ, i.e. the Institution Narrative.

In the East there was a similar but not identical development. John Chrysostom, who was contemporary with Ambrose, takes what appears to be a very similar line in his sermon *De proditione Iudae:*
> 'It is not a man that causes what is set forth to become the body and blood of Christ, but Christ himself who was crucified for us. The priest stands, fulfilling the form and saying these words; but the power and the grace is God's. "This is my body", he says. This saying transforms what is set forth. And as that utterance which said "Increase and multiply and fill the earth" was spoken once, but is effective for all time, enabling our nature to beget children; so this utterance, spoken once, renders the sacrifice complete on every altar in the churches from then until now and until his coming.'[3]

Does Chrysostom attribute the transformation of the elements ('what is set forth') to the words 'This is my body' as originally spoken by Jesus, or as repeated by the priest? Probably both: the recital of the Institution Narrative by the priest makes effective the grace promised at the Last Supper. But as we shall see, this is not the whole of Chrysostom's theology of consecration. The Institution Narrative has never had for

[1] *PEER* [1]p.99, [2]p.113.
[2] *In Ioann. Tract.* 80.3.
[3] 1.6 (J. P. Migne *Patrologia Graeca* 49, p.380).

the Eastern churches the unique status that it has been given in the West. Other parts of the eucharistic prayer share its importance.

The historic Roman Canon probably reached the main outlines of its final form about the time of Ambrose and Chrysostom, and we now turn to see what it has to tell us about the process of consecration (a word, incidentally, which it does not use). The underlying doctrine is nowhere explicitly expressed, but has to be deduced from the phraseology employed. Immediately before the Institution Narrative God is asked to make the offering

> 'blessed . . . and acceptable, so that it may become for us the body and blood of your beloved Son;'[1]

In the third paragraph *after* the Narrative it is said that those who have partaken at the altar will have received 'the most holy body and blood of your Son'. At some point between the first quotation (from the *Quam oblationem* paragraph) and the administration of the elements, the offering *has become* the body and blood. Before the Narrative the offering is referred to as gifts and sacrifices (*'dona'*, *'munera'*, and *'sacrificia'*); in the first paragraph after the Narrative as a victim (*'hostia'*), literally 'a sacrificed animal'. This seems to locate the change in the elements quite precisely: that is, at the recital of the Institution Narrative (*Qui pridie*).

For confirmation we may return to Ambrose:

> 'Perhaps you will say "My bread is common [bread]". But that bread is bread before the words of the sacraments; when consecration has been applied, from [being] bread it becomes the flesh of Christ. And by what words and whose sayings does consecration take place? The Lord Jesus's . . .'

Later he adds:

> 'The word of Christ has power to change everything.'[2]

Clearly by this time the Institution Narrative had become part of the eucharistic prayer. Indeed, it is already present in the anaphora of Hippolytus, where it does not have the effect of a later interpolation, but other early prayers, such as *Addai and Mari,* seem not to have included it in their original form, and some scholars hold that it was still not included at Jerusalem in Cyril's time (*c.* 349-386).

Gradually over the years the Narrative became the focus of theological exposition and popular devotion. The word 'transubstantiation' was first used by the Lateran Council of 1215; and sooner or later the question was bound to be asked 'When does it happen?' Thomas Aquinas laid it down that 'the sole and essential form for the consecration of the bread' is the words *Hoc est corpus meum,* and for the wine, from *Hic est calix* down to *remissionem peccatorum.*[3] Even if the rest of the Canon were to be omitted, as long as these words were

[1] *PEER* [1]pp.107-8 [2]pp.121-2.
[2] *PEER* [2]pp.98-9, [2]pp.112-3.
[3] *Summa Theologica* Q.78. Arts. 1, 3, 5, 6.

spoken, the elements would be consecrated. Transubstantiation takes place in each case in the last instant of the words being spoken. Thus the consecration of the bread is completed before that of the wine is begun. The 'moment of consecration' could scarcely be defined more stringently.

The same beliefs are reflected in the ceremonial of the time. Bishop Odo of Paris, who died in 1208, ordered his priests, when they began to recite the Narrative, to keep the host (i.e. the priest's wafer) breast-high,not visible by the people, until they reached *Hoc est corpus meum,* and then to elevate it so that all could see it.[1] The custom soon became universal, and was reinforced by the ringing of a bell. It was virtually the only action during the Canon that the congregation could see, and they believed that at that moment they were seeing their Maker. The conclusion cannot be escaped that, whatever refinements may have been devised by sophisticated theologians, in popular faith and practice the recital of the Institution Narrative came perilously near to being regarded as a magical incantation which produced miraculous effects by its mere utterance.

It was this kind of development against which the Reformers reacted most vigorously. Luther had the highest regard for the words of institution themselves, and compared them as placed in the Canon to the ark of God in the temple of Dagon. In his *Formula Missae* (1523) he directs that they are to be *sung,* and then goes on to say, 'The consecration ended, let the choir sing the Sanctus',[2] which shows clearly that he still regarded their recital as effecting consecration. Zwingli, Bucer, and Calvin, however, all have the Institution Narrative read as a lesson, which was probably its original function in the service. The whole Reformed attitude is summed up by Bucer when he writes in the Order for Cologne:

'The whole substance of this sacrament is contained in these words.'[3]

Whatever doctrine Cranmer may have intended to express in the Canon of 1549, with its studied ambiguities, there is no doubt that in the Book of 1552 he had given up any thought that the Institution Narrative effected any change in the bread and wine; he regarded the body and blood of Christ as eaten and drunk in the Supper 'only after an heavenly and spiritual manner'. This comes out clearly in the new formula of administration:

'Take and eat this in remembrance that Christ died for thee, and feed on him in thy heart by faith with thanksgiving;'

and in the rubric which says:

'If any of the bread and wine remain, the curate shall have it to his own use,'

clearly including what remained in the chalice and on the paten.

[1] J. Jungmann *The Mass of the Roman Rite* (ET, 1951) vol.2, p.207, n.29.
[2] *PEER* [1]p.124, [2]p.138.
[3] *PEER* [1]p.146, [2]p.160.

Cranmer's position was soon challenged. Bishop John Jewel wrote: 'We pronounce the same words of *consecration* that Christ pronounced.'[1]
But he in his turn was answered some sixty years later by Bishop Thomas Morton, who pointed out that Christ's words were not 'words of blessing and consecration', but 'words of direction', a point which is often lost sight of, even today. Sanctification of the elements, Morton says, is effected by the word of Christ *and* 'public blessing in prayer, which is more properly called consecration'.[2]

The revisers of 1662 made no significant change in the wording of the prayer, but they gave it a more traditional colouring by giving it the title *'The Prayer of Consecration'.* and adding a rubric after communion directing the veiling of *'the consecrated elements'.* The revival of the manual acts by indented rubric pinpointed the Institution Narrative as the moment of consecration:

> And here he is to lay his hand upon every vessel . . . in which there is any wine to be consecrated.'

Lastly, the curate may now have only the bread and wine that remains *un*consecrated: *'if any remain of that which was consecrated',* it is to be consumed in church. All this allows, without enforcing, a more Catholic interpretation of Cranmer's very Protestant prayer.

Seventeenth-century visitation articles likewise continue to speak of 'the words of consecration'; but, as Dr. Richard Buxton has shown, what all the Caroline divines meant by consecration was 'the setting apart for the sacred use of communion', *not* transubstantiation. The view of Hamon l'Estrange is typical, that 'the words of God's blessing, jointly with those of Christ's institution'[3], constitute the consecration. In the next century Daniel Waterland goes even further by saying that the Institution Narrative does not consecrate, but ratifies and seals the consecration effected by the prayers.[4] In short, the classical Anglican view is that the recital of the Institution Narrative guarantees that the effect of the eucharistic prayer will be what Christ intended.

Despite these authorities, it is probable that by *c.* 1900 the vast majority of Anglicans, evangelicals, and anglo-catholics alike, had come to hold the Roman view that the Institution Narrative possessed consecratory powers distinct from those of the rest of the Prayer of Consecration, much less any other part of the service such as the Preface and Sanctus. The historic Anglican view was lost to sight. By the 1920s, however, several branches of the Anglican Communion were engaged on the revision of the communion service. A revival of interest in the early liturgies had led to the rediscovery of the primacy of thanksgiving, and consequently to the belief that the whole eucharistic prayer effects consecration, and not any particular moment

---

[1] *Works* (Parker Society) 1, p.122.
[2] *Of the Institution of the Sacrament of the Body and Blood of Christ (1635)* pp.10-1. I owe this quotation and much of this section to Dr. R. F. Buxton's authoritative study *Eucharist and Institution Narrative* (1976).
[3] *Alliance of Divine Offices* (Library of Anglo-Catholic Theology) p.317.
[4] *A review of the Doctrine of the Eucharist* (1737) p.98 (ed. W. van Mildert).

or form of words within it. The South African bishops in particular held firmly to this belief in their revision, and it was also the theology which underlay the Prayer of Consecration in the English Book of 1928. Theodore Woods, then Bishop of Winchester, wrote:
'Evidently the fact that, so to speak, the act of consecration is spread over the whole prayer rather than limited to one formula is a matter of difficulty and regret to some . . . Personally, I think this is one of [the Book's] chief glories.'[1]

This was also the belief of the Church of England Liturgical Commission which began work in 1955, and it is exemplified in their communion services originally known as Series 2 and Series 3. In these services, for the first time in an English rite, the Preface and Sanctus are printed as intral parts of the eucharistic prayer, which is now specifically designated 'The Thanksgiving', though this title has more recently been discarded in the Alternative Service Book in favour of 'The Eucharistic Prayer'. The whole prayer is intended to form a unity, though this is masked when congregations fall to their-knees immediately after the Sanctus. In order to avoid suggesting a moment of consecration, Series 2, as drafted, had no manual acts at the traditional place; the two included in the authorized form were inserted later to meet a desire of the Church Assembly which was in direct contradiction of the theology of the prayer and the sequence of the four actions. Series 3 managed to escape any such contradictory intrusions, and placed its manual acts where they ought to be, the taking of the bread and wine *before* the thanksgiving, and the fraction after it. The text of Rite A preserves this treatment of the manual acts, but they are still to be found in Rite B, and an opening Note allows the use of the 'traditional' acts even in Rite A.

The new Roman eucharistic prayers, on the other hand, are still quite explicit about a moment of consecration, thus:
'On the night in which he was betrayed, *(he takes the host in both hands)* he took bread and, giving you thanks, he blessed, broke, and gave it to his disciples, saying: Take and eat of this, all of you: for this is my body, which will be given for you *(he shows the* consecrated *host to the people . . .).'*
This must be taken in the context of the rest of the prayers, but even so, it shows a remarkable reluctance to accept the theology of the early liturgies which have been so freely drawn upon for the structure of the prayers and for many isolated phrases. The American Episcopalian prayers also include a rubric directing a 'taking' in the middle of the thanksgiving, and even keep the Prayer Book phrase *'wine to be consecrated'.* The fact is that no major part of the Christian Church has yet worked out a theology of consecration which does justice to both the primacy of thanksgiving *and* the importance of the Institution Narrative, still less expressed it adequately and consistently in its liturgy in word *and* ceremonial. There is much work to be done here at all levels.

[1] R. C. D. Jasper (ed.) *Walter Howard Frere: His Correspondence* (1954) p.121.

6. REMEMBRANCE

Thus the original simple thanksgiving underwent two substantial modifications: first, the thanksgiving for creation virtually disappeared and the introduction of the Sanctus located the central action of the service in heaven; and secondly, the introduction of the Institution Narrative meant that consecration of the elements was associated with the Narrative rather than with thanksgiving. What, then, should follow the Narrative in the eucharistic prayer? In 1552 Cranmer produced a solution which has remained unique: the concluding words of the Narrative, 'in remembrance of me', are followed immediately, without even an Amen, by the words of administration, 'Take and eat this *in remembrance* that Christ died for thee'. This link was made much less obvious in 1559, when the 1549 formula, 'The body of our Lord Jesus Christ, which was given for thee, preserve thy body and soul unto everlasting life', was inserted before 'Take and eat . . .'. The 1662 revisers completed the process by adding an Amen to the main prayer.

Most of the early liturgies also picked up the word 'remembrance', but to introduce a new section of the prayer itself, which therefore has the technical name *'anamnesis',* to which, as we shall see, there is no exact English equivalent. So Hippolytus, after an unusual version of Jesus's words:

'when you do this, (you) make my remembrance.
Remembering therefore his death and resurrection . . .'[1]

Hippolytus's thanksgiving for redemption does not go beyond the Last Supper, so that his anamnesis carries on a natural chronological sequence. This is the one point in his prayer where there is a close verbal link with the Roman Canon; and in that prayer also there has been no previous mention of the passion and resurrection, so that it is quite appropriate to refer to them here.

In other Eastern liturgies the situation is more complicated. *St. Basil* has already got as far as the ascension before the Narrative, and so finds itself going over the same ground in the anamnesis. *St. John Chrysostom* loses the link altogether by omitting 'Do this in remembrance of me', so that the 'therefore' in 'Remembering therefore' has no antecedent. Other liturgies extend the list of events 'remembered' to include the second coming, which stretches the meaning of the word 'remember' rather far.

Or does it? The Egyptian liturgies, independent as usual, preserve what is probably the most ancient procedure by continuing the Narrative with St. Paul's comment, 'As often as you eat this bread and drink this cup, you proclaim the Lord's death until he come'. This they take to be part of Jesus's words, reading 'you proclaim *my* death until *I* come'. They then add the words 'and confess my resurrection'. The prayer continues:

'Proclaiming thus, Lord, the death of your only-begotten Son . . .
and confessing his resurrection and his ascension into heaven,
and looking for his glorious coming . . .'[2]

[1] *PEER* p.22.
[2] *PEER* [1]p.39, [2]p.44.

There is no problem about *proclaiming* the second coming.

All this suggests that the word 'remembrance' was understood in a wider sense than a mere 'calling to mind'. There is little agreement among scholars about its meaning, and this discussion will have to be highly selective. Joachim Jeremias has suggested that Jesus's words mean 'Do this that *God* may remember me', and adduces some evidence in support.[1] The idea of reminding God of his promises is certainly to be found in such passages as:

'You who put the Lord in remembrance, take no rest, and give him no rest until he establishes Jerusalem' (Isaiah 62.6-7).

Jeremias's interpretation has been challenged, but it continues to find champions.[2] It certainly fits in with the way the liturgies use the word, and leads on naturally to the medieval view of the mass as 'pleading' the sacrifice of Christ.

Dix, on the other hand, regarded it as meaning 'a "re-calling" or "re-presenting" before God,'[3] but in all three examples which he quotes from the Old Testament, what is re-called is the *sin* of the person concerned, which weakens the relevance of these passages to the interpretation of the Institution Narrative.

It was pointed out above that in the Psalms 'remembrance' implied proclamation, not mere recollection; and this is echoed by St. Paul when he writes 'you proclaim the Lord's death'. We have just seen how the Egyptian liturgies develop this idea. At first sight, the heart of the eucharist may seem a surprising place for proclamation. But in St. Paul's time, as in our own, uninstructed worshippers may well have been present, since the eucharist followed on the common meal; and he expressly says that prayer must be offered in an intelligible manner so that the 'plain man'may be able to say his Amen to the thanksgiving. (In more recent times we may compare John Wesley's view of Holy Communion as a 'converting ordinance'.) But even if only the faithful are present, as soon became the rule, there is still need of proclamation. So far the worshipping community has been *giving thanks* to God; now it turns to the 'genuine encounter' with him in the communion, and this is prepared for liturgically by reminding the faithful of the events associated with our salvation (also, if Jeremias is right, by reminding God). This produces some repetition, but in contrast with the Preface, the anamnesis is the utterance of the congregation. Indeed, in many liturgies, both ancient and modern, they are given a response to say at this point.

As regards the *content* of the anamnesis, there is a remarkable difference between the New Testament and the liturgies. Whereas St. Paul speaks only of proclaiming the Lord's death in 1 Corinthians 11,

[1] J. Jeremias (see p.3, n.1) pp.237-55.
[2] 'The "Institution Narratives" and the Christian Eucharist' in The Church of England Doctrine Commission *Thinking about the Eucharist* (1972) p.44.
[3] *The Shape of the Liturgy* p.161.

the liturgies from Hippolytus onwards with one accord add his resurrection, and most go further. It seems quite a natural procedure to add the resurrection to the subjects for remembrance: the 'genuine encounter in the present' is surely with the risen Lord rather than with him crucified, if a distinction must be made. St. Paul himself goes on from the proclamation of the Lord's death to that of his resurrection in chapter 15; and though he does not link this to the eucharist, in each case he makes it clear that he received it from the Lord. As a consequence, already in the Roman Canon the anamnesis has become the climax of the prayer, at which the offering of the consecrated elements is made in solemn phrases which almost overshadow the events of our salvation, and this emphasis on offering pervades the rest of the prayer. Accordingly, the whole concept of eucharistic offering must now be examined.

7. OFFERING

From the earliest days of Christianity the thanksgiving over the bread and the cup was expressed in sacrificial language. Warrant for this was provided, for example, by Psalm 116:
'I will offer you a sacrifice of thanksgiving: and call upon the name of the Lord' (Psalm 116.15).
and this was taken up in the epistle to the Hebrews:
'Let us continually offer up a sacrifice of praise to God, that is, the fruit of lips that acknowledge his name' (Heb. 13.15).
(Notice that the content of praise includes the name of God, as in the *berakah* tradition.) Justin Martyr can still write:
'Prayers and thanksgivings made by worthy men are the only sacrifices that are perfect and well-pleasing to God.'[1]
Behind his words probably lies a seminal verse in Romans:
'I beseech you, brethren, by the merci of God, to present your bodies as a living sacrifice, holy and acceptable to God, which is your spiritual worship.' (Rom. 12.1).
Thus Athenagoras, a little later, speaks of 'the lifting-up of holy hands' by Christians as 'a bloodless sacrifice and spiritual liturgy'.[2] This is perhaps the earliest appearance of the word 'bloodless', which is prominent in many liturgies, and in the form 'unbloody' had a new lease of life in this country in the eighteenth century. In Athenagoras it presumably means a verbal sacrifice as opposed to an animal. Origen, also, writes of the Christian 'continually offering bloodless sacrifices in his prayers to God'.[3]

But soon the phrase begins to widen its scope. By the end of the fourth century, it is clear that such phrases as 'the sacrifice of praise' or 'the bloodless offering' are no longer being used to describe the thanksgiving, but refer exclusively to the elements. In Cyril of Jerusalem, for instance, the gifts are referred to as 'the spiritual sacrifice, the bloodless offering', in clear distinction from the offering of thanks, as summed up in the Sanctus, which he has just described as 'spiritual hymns'. The transfer of meaning was easily accomplished, perhaps was inevitable, because of the juxtaposition of the offering of thanks with the presentation of bread and wine, already found in Justin. It was then a purely practical process for getting the elements from the people, who brought them, to the president, who was to give thanks over them.

But the ceremonial associated with it rapidly develops, and so does the theology. Already in Hippolytus, it is the deacons who receive the offerings from the people and present them to the bishop; 'and he, laying his hands on it . . . shall give thanks'; and the anaphora follows. Two small steps have been taken towards the medieval development of the offertory as an action of importance in its own right. There is a similar close connection between offering thanks and offering the gifts in the thought of Irenaeus, who sees the offering of bread and wine as an enacted giving of thanks. This is a natural extension of the concepts underlying the Jewish *berakah*. Both Justin and Irenaeus apply the

[1] *PEER* p.18.
[2] *Legatio* p.13.
[3] *Contra Celsum* p.8.21 (ET, H. Chadwick, p.467).

word 'eucharistia', 'thanksgiving', to the *thing* over which thanks have been given. Already the offering of the gifts is beginning to be given that priority over the offering of thanks which is such a prominent feature of the Roman Mass.

It is the combination of the idea of offering a sacrifice with the idea that the bread and wine *are* the body and blood of Christ in the fullest ontological sense that produces the theology which underlies the Roman Canon. Maurice Wiles puts it very clearly:

'If the elements *are* the body and blood of Christ and the offering *is* a sacrifice, then the eucharist as a whole must be a sacrificial offering of the body and blood of Christ. This concept we find explicitly affirmed in the teaching of Cyprian. But the composite idea thus created is in fact something very different from the ideas of the two . . . parts before they had been thus combined.'[1]

As a result of this combination of ideas, sacrificial language comes to dominate the Canon. Four times, God is asked to accept our offerings:

'We therefore pray and beseech you . . . to accept and bless these gifts, these offerings, these holy and unblemished sacrifices . . . which we offer to you . . .'

'Therefore, Lord, we pray you graciously to accept this offering made by us, your servants . . .'

'Vouchsafe . . . O God, to make this offering wholly blessed, approved, ratified, reasonable, and acceptable . . .'

(Notice the distant echo of Romans 12, here translated 'reasonable'.)

'Vouchsafe to look upon them [i.e. the gifts] with a favourable and kindly countenance, and accept them as you vouchsafed to accept the gifts of Abel, Abraham, and Melchizedek'.[2]

The whole Canon could almost be summed up in the words 'Accept our offering'. This is a far cry from the simple *'offerimus'* of Hippolytus. Thanksgiving has been confined to the Preface and Sanctus, thus breaking the close link which Irenaeus saw between thanking and offering, and substituting an equally close link between offering and a change in the elements.

Nor was this emphasis on offering confined to the Canon. During the Middle Ages a number of offertory prayers were added which anticipate the Canon, so similar is the language employed:

'Receive, holy Father . . . this unblemished offering which I . . . present to you . . . for my innumerable sins . . . for all who stand round, and for all faithful Christians, alive and dead . . .'

'We offer you, Lord, the cup of salvation and pray that . . . it may ascend in the sight of your divine majesty . . .'

'May our sacrifice be performed today . . . so as to please you . . .'

'Receive, holy Trinity, this offering which we offer you . . .'

'Pray, brothers, that my sacrifice and yours may be acceptable to God . . . May God receive the sacrifice from your hands . . .'[3]

[1] 'The Theological Legacy of St. Cyprian' in *Journal of Ecclesiastical History* 14 (1963) p.14; reprinted in *The Making of Christian Doctrine* (1967) p.122, and in *Working Papers in Doctrine* (1976) p.78.
[2] *PEER* [1]pp.106-8, [2]pp.120-2.
[3] *PEER* [1]pp.105-6, [2]pp.119-20.

These phrases could perfectly well come from the Canon itself; indeed, it is only the absence of the Institution Narrative that deprives them of equal consecratory power. (Hence the medieval name *'canon minor'*.) The same tendency is found in the East, though there it is held in balance with thanksgiving.

This emphasis on offering the elements, whether unconsecrated or consecrated, was totally unacceptable to the Reformers, who, almost to a man, excised *any* kind of eucharistic prayer from their services. The most prominent exception was Cranmer, and even he did not allow any offering of the elements; indeed, he specifically forbade any elevation. Even in 1549 he would only say:

'We *celebrate* and make here before thy divine majesty *with these thy holy gifts the memorial* which thy Son hath willed us to make.'

He was still able at that stage to define this action as 'our sacrifice of praise and thanksgiving'; but there is *no* offering of the gifts either before, during, or after the consecration. In his *Defence* he explains that there are only two offerings in the service; one is the sacrifice of Christ, which he offered himself; and the other is the Church's self-offering, to which Cranmer here applies the hard-worked phrase, a sacrifice of 'laud, praise, and thanksgiving'.[1] These offerings are still there in 1552, but the gifts and the memorial have gone. Cranmer restores the emphasis on *worthy* participation, which is prominent in Justin and Hippolytus, but had subsequently become peripheral. The quotation from Romans 12 had been picked up by Bucer, who gave it a prominent place in his services, and it was probably from him that Cranmer derived his phrase:

'Here we offer and present unto thee our self, our souls and bodies, to be a reasonable, holy, and living sacrifice.'

As might be expected, Laudians such as Cosin, L'Estrange, and Thorndike all argue that the eucharist involves 'the consecration of the elements, and presenting them up to God'; but they did not succeed in writing their theology into any actual liturgy. That achievement was left to the Nonjurors in their office of 1718. Here the anamnesis continues 'We offer to thee . . . this bread and this cup'. Under their influence the Scottish office of 1764 revives the 1549 and 1637 anamnesis and inserts the words 'which we now offer unto thee', printing them in capitals. From the Scottish book the phrase passes into the American (1790), and a similar one is found in the South African rite (1929). However, the English 1928 Book made no attempt to include it.

Given the Liturgical Commission's respect for Hippolytus, it is not surprising that when the Series 2 communion service appeared, it contained the words 'we offer unto thee this bread and this cup'.[1] The evangelical reaction was understandably vigorous. Equally firm was their refusal to accept any such comparable phrases as 'set before thee' or 'offer *with* this holy bread and cup'. After debates of unusual acrimony, the phrase was dropped in favour of:

'With this bread and this cup we make the memorial . . .'

which still stands in Rite B of the Alternative Service Book.

[1] *Defence* 5.3 (quoted in G. Dix *The Shape of the Liturgy* p.654).

No attempt was made to reinstate the original at any stage in the preparation of Series 3. Instead the irenic formula was adopted:
'With this bread and this cup we do this in remembrance of him;' and this was defined once more as 'our sacrifice of thanks and praise', which is patient of a Catholic interpretation. In the final revision which produced the communion services of the 1980 Book, this part of the anamnesis proved to be the most recalcitrant of the entire book. A prayer which both anglo-catholics and evangelicals can use must do full justice to the offering of Christ on the cross and the offering of the consecrated elements. Much depends on the choice of verbs, and even on which verbs are main verbs and which in subordinate clauses. The four Eucharistic Prayers offer the following solutions:

1. 'We remember his offering . . . we celebrate his sacrifice.'
2. As Series 2 above, but in modern English.
3. 'We celebrate this memorial of our redemption . . . we bring before you this bread and this cup.'
4. 'We offer you through him this sacrifice of praise and thanksgiving.'

'Bring before you' is now acceptable, and so is 'offer' when applied to praise and thanksgiving.

Elsewhere in the Anglican Communion the phrase has had a kinder reception. Since 1966 the Church in Wales has been happy to say:
'We do set forth . . . this bread of eternal life and this cup of everlasting salvation.'
In America the Episcopal Church also provides four different prayers:

A. 'We offer you these gifts.'
B. 'We offer our sacrifice of praise and thanksgiving.'
C. 'We . . . bring before you these gifts.'
D. 'Offering to you, from the gifts you have given us, this bread and this cup.'

North India has a good Cranmerian phrase:
'We set apart this bread and this cup.'

This controversy has, of course, no parallel in the Roman Catholic Church, which continues to use words of offering without any inhibitions: in Prayer II 'the bread of life and the cup of salvation'; in Prayer III 'this holy and living sacrifice'; and in Prayer IV, 'his body and blood' The new Roman offertory prayers, though widely used in Anglican services, are open to the same objection as their predecessors, of pre-empting the consecration, though they are more tactfully phrased. The English translation 'We have this bread to offer' is a very free rendering of the Latin, which has only *offerimus'*.

The last fifteen years have certainly seen a *rapprochement* both within the Church of England and *vis-à-vis* the Church of Rome. There is now hope that some day complete agreement may be reached.

---

[1] The phrase is actually quoted in the form found in *Apostolic Constitutions:* '. . . *this* bread and *this* cup'; Hippolytus has *'the* bread and *the* cup'.

8. EPICLESIS

After commemorating the work of the Father in creating the world and sending his Son, and the work of the Son in redeeming mankind and instituting the eucharist, the eucharistic prayer would naturally include some reference to the work of the Holy Spirit. In most early liturgies this takes the form of a petition to the Father to send his Holy Spirit either upon the worshippers, that they may receive the fruits of communion, or upon the bread and wine, that they may become the body and blood of Christ. Both kinds of epiclesis may be present in one prayer, either separately or combined. Or again, as in the historic Roman Canon and the Book of Common Prayer, there may be no explicit epiclesis at all, though in these cases the whole prayer may be regarded, in a sense, as a kind of epiclesis.

In most early liturgies the epiclesis arises out of the anamnesis as a request for 'the divine response to the Church's obedience to Christ's command'.[1] In Egypt, however, it arises out of the Sanctus, picking up the words 'full of your glory', and asking God to 'fill this sacrifice with a blessing through your holy Spirit'. In two prayers the petition at this point already asks for the transformation of the elements. Later, the Egyptians added a second epiclesis in the more usual place, and this double epiclesis may have influenced the Roman Canon. It certainly provides a precedent for the new eucharistic prayers.

The epiclesis on the congregation appears to have been the first to be included, but during the fourth century, in parallel with developments in the theology of the Spirit, the epiclesis on the elements comes to the fore. The verbs used gradually intensify the purpose; first, the Spirit is to bless and sanctify the elements; then, to show them or make them to be the body and the blood; and finally, to change them. This last is the crucial verb, implying a developed doctrine of the Spirit as well as a consecration. Cyril of Jerusalem writes (c. 350-386):
> 'Everything that the holy Spirit has touched has been sanctified and changed.'[2] (my italics).
Even then, only the Liturgy of *St. John Chrysostom* and the Coptic version of *St. Mark* are bold enough to use the word 'change'.

Neither John Chrysostom in his sermons nor Cyril discusses the relation of the descent of the Spirit to the effect of the Institution Narrative, though the former speaks of the Spirit's advent and *completion* of the sacrifice. There is an internal incoherence here which they do not attempt to explain, perhaps were not even aware of. For them the consecration took place during the anaphora, which included the Institution Narrative and the epiclesis; and it did not occur to them to restrict the time of consecration to either particular moment. This refusal to particularize has persisted in Orthodox theology to the present day. For example, at the Great Entrance the unconsecrated

---

[1] W. J. Grisbrooke in J. G. Davies (ed.) *A Dictionary of Liturgy and Worship (1972)* p.15.
[2] *PEER* [1]p.53, [2]p.58; cf. [1]p.80; [2]p.90.

bread and wine then carried in have already the status of 'holy icons', and so may rightly be the objects of adoration; and this, before the anaphora has even begun.

The idea of the Spirit's descent being for the benefit of the congregation was never completely lost to sight. All the medieval Eastern liturgies ask that the Spirit may come 'upon *us*' as well as upon the gifts, and specify the fruits of communion which it is hoped he will provide. Those which are asked for most often are forgiveness of sins, strengthening of faith, union with the rest of the faithful, sanctification, and eternal life.

In the West the prayer developed along different lines. Whether the Roman concern with offering led to the extrusion of an epiclesis that was originally there, or the lack of an epiclesis led to the stress on offering, it is not now possible to say. The two ideas are not easily combined. In the West the movement tends to be upwards rather than downwards. The offering, whether of prayer or of gifts, is to be carried up to the *heavenly* altar by an angel, whereas in the East the holy Spirit is to descend to the *earthly* altar and sanctify what has been set on it. The Western approach avoids any difficulty about the relative efficacy of the Institution Narrative and the epiclesis, but leads all too easily to an over-schematic insistence on a moment of consecration. From the Western point of view an epiclesis *before* the Institution Narrative is preferable, since the Narrative can then be regarded as the moment of the Spirit's operation. If a consecratory epiclesis follows the Narrative, the latter's function is less obvious.

As is well-known, Cranmer included an epiclesis of a kind in the 1549 Canon, and before the Institution Narrative at that, just as the Roman liturgists were to do four hundred years later. But since he radically altered the passage in 1552, there is little point in discussing here what he had meant by it in 1549. He may have introduced it as a means of detaching the moment of consecration from the Institution Narrative, and thus preparing for the strictly non-consecratory prayer of 1552. In the latter he substituted the clause:
'Hear us, O merciful Father . . . and grant that we, receiving these thy creatures of bread and wine, according to thy Son our Saviour Jesus Christ's holy institution, in remembrance of his death and passion, may be partakers of his most blessed body and blood.'
This is an epiclesis addressed to the Father, with no mention of the Spirit, and including a vestigial anamnesis.

However, the story of the 1549 epiclesis does not end in 1552. The Reformed tradition regarded an epiclesis as essential, and in the seventeenth century the Scottish Presbyterians began to add one to the form in the Book of Common Order. Consequently, the ill-fated Scottish Prayer Book of 1637 was able to revive the 1549 epiclesis without arousing opposition. The presence of an epiclesis is predictable in the numerous liturgies of the eighteenth century based on the Eastern anaphoras, of which the Scottish rite of 1764 is the best-known example. In this service the epiclesis follows the Institution

Narrative, and has remained there until the present day, though the wording has been somewhat altered. The American Prayer Book inherited it from the Scottish, and also retained it without revision until recently. These two rites form the nucleus of a whole family of Anglican communion services which pray specifically for the consecratory action of the Holy Spirit in terms derived ultimately from the East.

In England itself the introduction of an epiclesis was one of the most hotly debated points in the lengthy discussions that eventually produced the 1928 Prayer Book. It would have come after the Institution Narrative, though Bishop Frere put forward the idea of allowing it either after or before. In recent years some kind of epiclesis at some place in the eucharistic prayer has become almost universal, and it is therefore surprising that Series 2 did not have one until it was revised in 1976; neither did Series 3 as originally drafted (unless the words 'renew us by your Holy Spirit' be counted as one). The words 'by the power of your Holy Spirit' were added by the General Synod, before the Institution Narrative, and caused no trouble at all. This was in strong contrast to the controversies of the 1920s and the contemporary *fracas* over offering. It would be wearisome to multiply examples: the essential point is that now throughout the Anglican Communion one of the chief weaknesses of the Prayer Book has been remedied.

The similar weakness in the Roman Canon has been rectified in a similar way. Prayer I, the old Canon, is still left without an epiclesis, but each of the other three has two, a consecratory one before the Institution Narrative and a congregational one after. The same is true of the first three prayers in the Alternative Service Book, though the second epiclesis in the first two prayers is very slight; and in Prayer IV there is no 'congregational' epiclesis at all. Prayer III makes some amends with an eloquent appeal to
'gather into one in your kingdom all who share this one bread and one cup . . .'
The American Prayer Book, with long tradition behind it, has epicleses on the gifts and on us in Prayers A, B, and D after the Narrative; Prayer C has a consecratory epiclesis before, and none after. Once more, a notable advance has been made in ecumenical agreement; and once more, work remains to be done to make that agreement total.

9. FRACTION

The third of the four actions is the breaking of the bread. This has no counterpart with the wine, though reference could easily have been made to 'pouring'. Nor was the breaking originally intended as a symbol of the crucifixion. The word 'broken' in the Authorized Version is a late addition. The Fourth Gospel does not mention Jesus's breaking of the bread in the Feeding of the Five Thousand, and goes out of its way to emphasize that 'a bone of him shall not be broken'. So, although 'the breaking of the bread' seems to have been the Church's first name for the eucharist, it is best seen as purely preparatory. This has been made clearer in the Alternative Service Book by moving the fraction nearer to the administration, and by a slight change in the Institution Narrative. Cranmer's version, 'and when he had given thanks, he brake it', presents the thanksgiving as a preparation for the fraction. The ASB, reading:

'[he] took bread and gave you thanks;
he broke it and gave it to his disciples . . .'
corrects the balance.

10. PARTICIPATION

'Giving' implies 'receiving'; and the process whereby the bread and the wine become the body and the blood of Christ is not complete until the elements have been received. An Orthodox theologian writes:

'The bread and the wine do not have value in themselves: it is given to them by the fact that they are *consumed* by and in the Body of Christ. In the East . . . the fact that those who are already members of Christ's Body communicate, is just as important as the consecration of the material elements.[1]

Roman Catholic thought concurs in this insight. While Christ's offer of himself does not depend on the faith of the believer, it is only *complete* when it is received *in faith.* Karl Rahner makes the very significant comment:

'The Reformation doctrine that the act of faith constitutes the presence of the Lord, although it was false and heretical when applied to the individual, can have a good Catholic sense when said of the Church as a whole.'[2]

[1] N. Nissiotis quoted by J. McKenna *Eucharist and Holy Spirit* (1975) p.184.
[2] 'The Word and the Eucharist' in *Theological Investigations* 4 (1966) p.285.